Unsigned Epitaph

Collected Poems Of
NilavroNill Shoovro

Edited By
Alicja Kuberska

Published By
NIGHTinGALE

2020

Unsigned Epitaph

Editor: Alicja Kuberska

Cover Designer : Suvra Bhattacharya

ISBN: 978-1-67816-311-2

Copyright: Suvra Bhattacharya

2020

PREFACE

Poetry is a means to transcend our personal visionary limitations to reach the cultural extensions of our traditions and inheritance in our ever-changing present time. Poetry also keeps us constantly pushing towards the fast approaching future. Poetry communicates the emotions evolved from the nervous system of the poet to the very inner soul of the readers, without which a poem remains unfinished. Poets use new metaphors, putting things in new perspectives in an attempt to make us see and feel things as if for the first time. They renew the old in their own styles to keep us attached with our traditions and heritage only to create a new dimension for the future, paving the present in a continuous manner.

Is poetry the supreme expression of the noblest human emotions: of love and sympathy; of awareness of the infinite value of life; of the realizations of the eternal truth through the strokes of individual talents of creative genius? Yes poetry is all these together in a single volume of human brilliance! And a poet's life is the extension of human consciousness into the eternal essence of life and sympathy! His soul belongs to the future as well as to the present of his own time with the cultural heritage of his predecessors. So a true poet lives not only in his contemporary time but also in the time future with his cultural heritage projecting the eternal essence of human sympathy and consciousness.

Actually, as an artist or poet or writer we have a legacy of our past which keeps alive in our present and becomes eternal in our future. This is the tradition of literary genius of which we are the torch bearer. That doesn't necessarily mean that the individual talent only repeats itself in every age; on the contrary, individual talent illuminates the tradition in its unique personality and creative genius! The eternal expresses itself through this creative genius in every age. We in our limited capacity try to reflect this constant rediscovery of our individual talents in our relation to this literary tradition!

And the tradition of art and philosophy keeps our literature modern and alive in every age. We rediscover ourselves as an individual through our relation to this tradition. And the comparative re-evaluation of the eternal realizations shapes our individual genius as an artist or poet. It is the magic of poetry which every poet wants to live with, to explore and to put an individual signature of brilliance into it.

Unsigned Epitaph

BOOK 1

Dreams Die Fast

And at last the indomitable world
Was unfolding in my palm.
All the skies were merging
Into my blue.
All the seas drowned
Into my passions.
All the stars melted
In my vein.
And then I had recruited Time.
To keep the show rolling.

In our everyday meeting
We discussed how to form
The blood the red one!
I told the primordial atom
To diffuse every pain into love.

The blood will run the world.
And it happened just as I thought.
All the cosmic nights
With their different angles-
Tried to warn us, reminding-
That blood was forbidden.
Forbidden from the very start.

Before the onset of every Big bang,
They tried the same.
In my first dream
I felt those passionate kisses
Beneath those locked eyes.

Holding the breath together
Believing in each other!

Mesmerized! That I became.
So, blood was inevitable to form.
But it became bloodier
In every battle from the
Neolithic time.

So, the primordial atom
Sheds tears accusing me
For Everything.
From greed to power.
From hate to violence.
From deceit to lies.

Now when I see them walking inside.
Inside the four corners of the
Security Council.
Determined to uphold their lies,
When blood is shedding bitter tears
In my palm, I know,
Dreams die fast.

26th August 2014
NilavroNill Shoovro

The Birth

I am the only one, all alone
With none to be substituted.
I am the solace of the sufferers
Everywhere around everything.

I know the secret numbers
To unlock the mind.
I know the dark chamber
Of the soul in eternity.

I overwhelmed the waves of
Our history, surviving along
The time scale of nuisance
Standing erect over the debris

Of beliefs from the time past
To the time future.
Circling Around all the lost hopes.
For I alone know the secret.

Beneath the surface reality
And above the virtual designs
Of hopes and aspirations.
Of anguish and humiliation.

I'm the sole witness from the beginning-
Of the story to the never ending
Rituals of Eternity, day in and
Day out. All around the inside.

Stars will fade out. Time will Pass.
Life will stop crying for-
The first breath of the fresh- Dawn.

Yet I will be there.

For you, for you alone in a
Lonely world of peace and trust.
For the poetry of love-
Just in two eyes. For my birth!

NilavroNill Shoovro

The Deep Secret

she was talking in undertone
like the old hermits of the
Buddhist Monastery

not to prove any algorithm
or to put forward hypothesis
of social revolution

she was there with her
gentle smile and her bare arms
moving like gentle breeze

not like the smiling bureaucrats
shaking the cold hands
before the secret deals

she was looking around
along the time scale of eternity
like the twinkling stars

from the distant galaxies
around the summer nights;
serene, poised like the Pacific

her looks were quite different
from the performers
playing with the power

behind the closed doors
after the success of
summit meetings here and there

she was there engrossed in

deep collaboration with
the forthcoming embryos

like the painter over her canvas
playing with all the colours
to make one of her own

one without any blood spot
one without any inflicted pain
one without any human grief

NilavroNill Shoovro

Fragments of Revolution!

like the dark side of the moon
i wished your attention.
alone but not fragile!
doomed but not hopeless!
casual but not reluctant!
yet:
reciting- warfare to adulteries;
preaching- peace treaty to abortions;
teasing- prophet to pauper;
you kept me waiting.
authentication of truth is not valid
like your mascara and false eyelashes any more.
but leaflets of secret circles
squares and triangles promise your love-
for the believers of dream around!
like the dark side of the moon
i wished your attention
not for the mosaic of your stories.
but to see how long you can carry on
.... your Excellency!

NilavroNill Shoovro

Down Memory Lane

within the range of your eyes
with the residue of love
like the mist descending
in your heart:
-is my walk!
and still I'm walking
with the lonely steps
of every single person on earth.
-from down memory lane......

is love haunted always by betrayal?
like dusk masking the sky?
or we make the error to fathom
each other's terror?
decide to cover up the past
with the blankets of disbelieves!
-from down memory lane.....

walking down the earth we look around;
for our inward sun
with dying shadows
or mourn over
our lost desires:
like the lonely desert
for a drop of primordial rain!
-from down memory lane...

NilavroNill Shoovro

When We Dance Together

During the monsoon, all my raindrops drag me
Towards the fast lane of memories.
Taking with all the skies and the stretched blues.
Feeling not like the dead warriors
But the first saint under the young sun.
One day when we were dancing together
Hovering on the untold secrets of the battle fields
All the dead pawns of world history
From the past to the present
Mimicked us under the tone.

I have seen the first smile of the antithesis of God.
Not only the everyday hypothesis lies
But all the dead philosophies under the religious cult
Fooled us every time we thought
We have found Him.

Talking about the story of love all my raindrops
One day came to me.
We were so proud of each other
Touching the pride of faith;
Yet all the dead souls of cathedrals
Mimicked us underneath.

And then I have seen the first smile
Of the whispering secretes of life
Drawing the first sketch of the antithesis of God,
During our everyday monsoon.

27th April 2014
NilavroNIll Shoovro

The Dark Passages

Sleepless nights and the
Monsoon rain, drops after drops
Sharing little secrets besides
Greenwood trees. All alone!

I, like the other homo sapiens
Behind the closed doors with
Abandoned theories of truth
In conversation with myself.

Under all the hidden floors
History with frozen steps
May start its own story
Hushed and covered up!

The obvious is not difficult to fathom!
But the herocs had
Different mosaics, in their
Minutes of lies. All along!

All the dark secrets with
Their rhymes and rhythms
Had tried to wipe out the truths
Yet sleepless nights prevail.

I, along with the passage of time
Besides the Greenwood trees
Try to fathom this human race
Like the primordial truth!
25th August 2014
NilavroNill Shoovro

After The Holocaust

Here I am,
The last man survived
Nobody left to console
None to share the pain
The only fool to withstand
The holocaust

It is raining since
The last bullet fired
Perhaps to wash out
Human sins
Till a single drop of
Dead blood remains

Feeling ashamed
Of all the memories
Feeling guilty
Of human legacy
Feeling relieved
From war and peace

Here I am,
With myself only
Alone and lonely
And ashamed of myself
Being the last Human species
Trespassing the earth!

NilavroNill Shoovro

Back To Square One

So, I have borrowed few words
No, not from the dictionary of civilization
Yet civilized enough in their own terms

At first, they observed my intentions
Diving deep into my desires and design
Perhaps to measure my honesty or hypocrisy

The day was bright as usual like our lies
Everywhere the newspapers were shouting
As much as they have been instructed

And I was waiting for the words
To guide me through my convictions
As I have been taught by the leaders of the nations

To my surprise the words started to disassemble
Into the alphabets of the ancient histories
In the middle of our conference

And suddenly even the alphabets
Started to dissolve into an unknown silence
That had never heard of

July The 29th 2018
NilavroNill Shoovro

Before The Revolution

Angry nights of solitude
Blank faces of nightmares
Voiceless pain of memories
Everything is so crucial

Everything is so fine tuned
With each other's like the
Ecosystem in and around
All are in perfect harmony

And I alone lonely along with me
Broken dreams and failed desires
Fractured faiths and buried beliefs,
Like the hermits walking on

Time has crumbled around
The space and Eternity~
Like the wounded soldiers
In the battlefields, in wars

Still I'm walking barefooted
Praying for new hopes
Around the unseen horizon
To meet with someone like me
      Someday... somehow …

13th October' 2018
NilavroNill Shoovro

End of The Civilization

My
Words and letters
With Your
Symbols and sentences
Sometimes
Moving up sometimes down
Or being pushed backwards
By our adversaries
Amidst our dreams forward
Disclosing emotions
      Desire and despair
With precision of human souls
From the ruins of dead dynasties

Poets and the storytellers alike
With their whimsical wisdom
Often make the blunder

(Like the warriors at the front
Believing they are the chosen one
To end the war for once and all)

      That their words will bring
      Sympathy Love and gratitude
      Dissolving nights into dawn

Yet on the other side of the spectrum
All my words and letters
With all your symbols and sentences
Remain devastated like the defeated
And destroyed squadrons in the battlefields

Only the hope of incarnation of God

Remains alive in human prayers
Amidst the ruins of my words and letters
With your symbols and sentences

July the 25th 2018
NilavroNill Shoovro

For The Next Millennium

It was dark
In the middle of the night
The lonely stars
Far away from each other's
Like the divorced couples
Were silent
Listening to the primordial music

Time and eternity
Together were playing with the chords
The silhouette of our dead souls
Were dancing in silence
Finding each other's
In their beloved arms

Each step
Was measured with
Our forlorn grief
Yet rhythmic in accord
 With the human dreams

Defeated yet not in vain
The night was overwhelmed
With both the pains and pangs
Of the primordial womb

Unfolding once again
To fulfil the human dreams
Of love and compassion

Then the alphabets will take over
Designing the vowels and the consonants

For the next millennium

August The 15th 2018
NilavroNIll Shoovro

Denying The Graveyard

They have crossed the line in dark
Like the ghosts coming out of the
Coffins one by one denying the graveyard

I have seen them almost everywhere
Crossing the borders sailing off
The turbulent seas in boats

During the heavy bombardment
During the famine or economic crisis
During the onslaught of globalization

They are not living being like others
They are only the numbers in millions
Heads counting heads over heads

They have no right to question
They have no right to demand
They have no right to fight

The members of the Security Council
The leaders declaring the wars
The profiteers of war industries

All are watching their movements
Briefing the press every day's lies
Before going off to bed in peace

October The 6th' 2018
NilavroNIll Shoovro

None To Face The Trial

None to face the trial …. but
All are busy to accuse one another
The battlefield is silent like desert
Hope you are still waiting for a start

People are marching ahead you know
Hoping for an oasis still
None to lead them this time
None to mislead though

They have come through enough
Paving the history with blood
They have learnt to disbelief
The leaders and their bluff

This time I am not waiting
For my poems to reopen
Like the saints or prophets
Drawing hope in vain

11th December' 2019
NilavroNill Shoovro

Opera of The Gods

No, I have nothing more to say
All my instruments are silent now
The chorus of the body and mind
Stopped in the middle of the show

No more audiences to follow
Applauses are dying very fast
Skylines are beaming in joy
As the clouds have retired at last

What has been good?
Or what has been not
What should have been done?
Or what should have been not

All these offstage doubts
Almost eternal human cries
Make my words weaker
And my poem dies

Yet my readers should know
The opera of the Gods is not finished over
Human cries may die
But the songs will continue to hover

July The 23rd 2018
NilavroNill Shoovro

Song of Palestine

I was there sleeping
Murdered with my wound
Like all the dead souls
In Palestine around

Even the blood frozen
Became history of the land
Millions of dead souls
Are glittering through the sand

Blank faces of my pains
The agonies on and on
The mist over the dead vision
All were in unison…

To escape from the death
To revolt against the goons
To fight for my voice
To win our freedom soon

August The 29th' 2018
NilavroNill Shoovro

The 21st Century Syndrome

Along the empty corridors
Silent eyes keep on spreading
The silence…
The frozen masks of peace
The dumb notes of harmony
The dead words of oath
Are marching ahead of time

The starved children of war
The dead civilians
Within the missile range
The naked women, raped
And sold in the market
Everyone knows it better
The price of living

In this lonely hour of insanity
In this empty crowd, thrashed
Shadows of bygone revolutions
How can I stand alone?
Wouldn't you come and save my words?
Forbidden, as they unfold the truths
Forbidden, as they stand alone…

27th November' 2018
NilavroNill Shoovro

The Fight

words too are insufficient
to unearth the whole truth
broad day light is not enough
to see the invisible
our love is too feeble
to fight against all wars
ground realities are too insane
to preach the peace
I must say, I am too insignificant
to convince you all these
yet all my words like
the shadows of our past following you

too many heroes had lost
their battle
too many epics
had failed
words didn't gain anything
other than personal pain
yet I'm here
even beyond my dream
counting every moment
of human times
stars may fade out one day
still I'll continue my fight….

October The 3rd' 2018
NilavroNill shoovro

The Promised Land

Somehow the lights were fizzled out
In the middle of our mutual understandings

Both of us felt left out in the dark of the night
Especially when cold wind was all around

It was really a difficult situation to handle
When none of us was sure about the other

Yet we remain there waiting with patience
For the silence to dissolve into the beliefs

That time will bridge up the alien territories
And we would discover the land in between

July The 20th 2018
NilavroNill Shoovro

The Proposal

This world of mine,
I know remains alone
As I have anchored myself
In loneliness deep inside

Deep inside of the embryo
I am all alone like the Universe
Eternal as usual Timeless though
Standstill and silent ever

The waves of histories
Down the ages and the ages to come
Remain there outside
Here I rule my world

No, I'll never ask you to poke
Nor even send proposals
Yet if you ever decide
I may open my world for you

**July The 18th 2018
NilavroNill Shoovro**

Waiting for A Miracle

Sleepless nights and desolate mornings
Intense longing for someone
With the master key to unlock
The deadlock memories of another time

With the lonely skies of daydreams
Like the mirages of hope at the bend of the
Distant journeys under the dark shadows …
This night still I'm waiting for a miracle

The wounded nights like the broken chords
Remain silent whispering in grief and agonies
Like the exhausted whirlwind after the storm
Lamenting for the memories, dead and bygone

Yet faint shadows like dew drops would emerge
In between insanity and hope like the pale moon
Behind the overtaking dark clouds…
Like your smile encouraging me for a miracle

August The 28th' 2018
NilavroNill Shoovro

With The Soul Face To Face

Now I'm gliding through
Like the dead Phoenix
Nothing to be worried about
No more anxiety or planning

They have taken away the body
To the morgue tagged my name
On it, rituals are to be performed
According to the norms and oaths

It's a great relief to be alone
With the soul face to face
In the dark chamber of
The confession box

Nothing to hide from
No more usual lies
Or counterfeit truths
To establish human glory

August the 20th' 2018
NilavroNill Shoovro

A Woman Or A Poetry Line

It was late at night as usual
With the burning moon inside
Setting the timeline ablaze

Human words with pauses
And the social norms inbuilt
Often missed the right moments

Even the sea waves, eternal
Never failed to embrace
Within the time-frame

Shadows of buried couples
Still waking side by side
Yet to hit the right words

So, I like those failed poets
With the upturned words
Betrayed the burning moon inside

Again, it is late at night as usual
Even the moon is burning
Setting the timeline ablaze

But my words are mute still
Never know how to convince
A woman or a poetry line…

10th December' 2019
Nilavronill Shoovro

Around The Corner of Eternity

(I know she is too busy
With her works and admirers
Often rewriting her verses again
I wish I met her once during
Any poetry meets years before)

Walking around fancy dreams
Day in and day out
Through the lonely corridors
Of solitude, like the desolate sailor
Of the pacific

The vagabond words march on
Around the circle of silence
Like the impatient whirlwind
With the failed attempted
To anchor hopes anywhere

Temptations loom large
To find out any corner
Harbouring desperate desires…
With the pounding heart beats
Just waiting for someone's footsteps

Solitary tales of lonely shadows
Hidden pangs of unspoken loves
Weave around autobiographies
Of Sleepless nights and hostile wait
Around the corner of eternity…

17th November' 2019
NilavroNill Shoovro

Footprints of Revolution

Footprints of time past
Along with the memories
Of war and cries
      Silent, ageless; melancholic

Words with syllables
Deceptive in nature
With the mask of peace
      Wrote the scripts as usual

Footprints of time present
Perform the act as expected
Even with the dream to excel beyond
      Future waits in distant

Smiles with promises
Secret meetings behind the curtains
Keeping the mosaic hidden
      Formulates deceptions anew

Footprints of time future
Whisper in advance, desperate
Restless to fight back
      For you and I and the others…..

I'm waiting for you
We would wait for them
To embrace the footprints of time future
      In love in humanity

14th April' 2019
NilavroNill Shoovro

Beneath The Treasure Mountains

Beneath the treasure mountains
You can hear their whispers, still
Like the sound of the last breath
Preparing themselves finally
…………………..for their own grave

Let them die peacefully if you can
With all their hopes for a better life
Like the wings of the migrant birds
Like the dreams of the humiliated
…………………..for the final peace

Most of us are like them, in the queue
Hoping still to escape the riddle
The owners are happy and jubilant
Proud of their treasure mountains
…………………..for their exploits

Because of the riddle they set
Because we love to survive
Because we need to believe
Because we like to dream
…………………..they defeat us each time

Beneath the treasure mountains
History unfolds with the same old story
Philosophers and the prophets alike
Remain perplexed with
…………………..their own words and lines,

(they don't even know why)

16th February 2019
NilavroNill Shoovro

Dialects of Evolution

The night had settled down
With silent dreams
Lovers were busy like the
Bees around the hives

My fingers were strolling
As usual through her attire
Caring and enjoying simultaneously
She knew my intentions well

Provoking my sensations
With her silent smile
Circling around my warmth
Like the rainbow after the drizzle

Speechless moon was watching
Our shadows wriggling around
Hovering over each other
Hypnotized in passions and desire

The night was in full swing
No more talks of war and peace
No more conferences
On conflicts here and there

We were engrossed in each other
We remain enclosed in flesh
We didn't notice anything yet
We never cared about anything else

Night wind was blowing gentle
Calm soothing, lovers on bed
Her lips and mine, tender touches

Painting the night in order

Forgetting everything else
Disorders and the anarchies
Around the everyday life
We remained innocents

People were crying in agony
Like the rheumatic patients
With the shattered beliefs
Limping in shaken steps

Our memories were faded out
No pain no grief no revolution
Only the intercourse remained
True to the dialects of evolution

30th April' 2019
NilavroNill Shoovro

Inside The Borders

Sea waves
Fresh air
Blue skies
Flying birds
    are not like us
International borders
With arms and ammunitions
Immigration policies
With rubberstamps and signatures
    rule supreme over our steps
Clouds with the raindrops
Rivers along the downstream
Daylight over the horizon
Even dreams of the pauper
    are not like us
Scriptures and the manifestos
Religions and the politics
Traditions and the heritage
Egos and the prejudices
    control our intentions

We remain confined…
We remain divided…
We remain dwarf…
We remain incomplete…

5th May' 2019
NilavroNill Shoovro

Last Words

You'll find me counting my words
In my secret manifesto
Written well before my sentence
You may feel the scorching irritations
The unfolding stresses of tensions
And the pain sustaining tragedies

Of human love and compassion
Of exploitations and lies
Of power and manipulations
You may argue with the alternatives
The pros and cons of the plans
The mosaic of the future

Designed by one sentenced soul
Paved with determination
And desire to uphold only the truth
Of endless possibilities of man
And his tireless Endeavour
To light up the dawn ….

8th April' 2019
NilavroNill Shoovro

Lying Dead As Usual

On a day when even the moon
Will remain asleep in the dark
I will die alone with none but myself

A day that nobody will care to remember
For any reasons or other nor even may notice
A day with the breaking news misspelled

While the roads will be busy with the traffic
Politicians with their lies and smile on the face
Stocks will go up and down in regular rhythm

All the road shows will continue as usual
Fooling the crowds and uniting the people
Driving them around the whirlwind

I'll remain dead with the scattered flies
Hovering upon their new found treasure
With full of zeal and happiness

On a day like any day today or tomorrow
Or even the last day gone ashtray
I'll die like rotten apple fallen downwards

You may smell the air with suffocating pain
Or may wonder what has gone wrong
Under the open sky suddenly

No, you'll find everything remains the same
From time immemorial towards the eternity
Even with the dead body of a stranger

Lying alone along with the forgotten history

Of the crowds, fooled enough to believe
The lies and the uproar of their times

Just like me or anyone else
Of today or tomorrow now or then
As ever as long with the usual countdown

8th April' 2019
NilavroNill Shoovro

Not To Wake Up Anymore

We are the blind men
With silent eyes
Empty dreams
And strange darkness
Around the mind

We are the blind men
We do not want to see
The madness all around
We do not want to look
Forward or backward

We are the blind men
With frozen beliefs
Upturned faiths
And broken oaths
Around our deeds

We are the blind men
We would like to be
The dumb and the deaf
Like the statues standstill
All around space and time

We are the blind men
With dead hopes
Broken shadows
And spineless movements
Around the history

We are the blind men
We would be delighted
To remain blind ever

Not to wake up anymore
Not to revolt anywhere

23rd June' 2019
NilavroNill Shoovro

Preparing for A Duet Concert

Silent trees and voiceless sky
Over head with blank face
Like the untold stories of
Dead love, yet suffering

Escaping from
The deadlocked nights
Like the caged bird
With the wounded heart

Yet crying inside deep
Bleeding still with pain
Running wild into
The dark memories

Insane nights with the
Dumb stars blinking
Down memory lane
Following like the shadows.

Yet, you may like to
Step into the fresh dawn
Like the singing bird
Preparing for a duet concert……

20th June' 2019
NilavroNill Shoovro

Of Human History

It is time to face the mirror
It is time to retrospect
It is time to meet the truth
It is time to know thyself

Not all the forgotten tales
Are dead or vanished
Not all the dead faces
Have lost their stories

War and terror are synonymous
Warriors are murderer too
Battlefields are the graveyards
Of love and peace, dignity

**14th May' 2019
NilavroNill Shoovro**

Soldiers' Paradise

Bodies pile up
With wounded blood
Mute, silent like lost histories,
Abandoned forever

No more parades
No more attacks on enemies
No more following commands
      Blindfolded without debates

Eyelids will not blink ever
Lips will never find a kiss
Frozen hopes are gone with bloods
      Yet the battlefields roar

Silent whispers mad in pain
Crushed believes lame in faith
Lost tears dripped in passion
      Will roam around chained in death

Bodies will pile up
With wounded bloods
With untold stories, like the
      Canvas never attempted

Silent prayers for the peace
Ardent beliefs of a God
Every bullet fired on targets
      Keep on lying everyday

27th August' 2019
NilavroNill Shoovro

The Rebellion!

Empty dreams are howling around
Love has taught me how to sustain pain

The headlines are crying for revenge
Peace treaties only prolong the game

No matter how you see the picture
Your voice would be lost in vain

Or you can dance along with the time
To get the limelight and the fame

There is no fairy tale that I can narrate
To give you joy or boost up the hope

Nor I can dishearten you with the facts
True, yet naked in shame down the roads

Or you can still play Nero's violin
If you wish, you have the scope

But for me, I'm alone: Empty dreams
Are dancing around the silent swords!

5th March' 2019
NilavroNill Shoovro

The Price

With the forgotten ink
I'm here, trying hard
To light up secret words

Like the scattered blood
Of war victims
Draws out the value of life

Forget the wasted inks
Forget the wasted blood
Forget the wasted moments

Does ethereal language of life
Like the ice ages
Washout human sins ever?

My pocket is full of tricks
To win your heart
For today and tomorrow

You are no different either
With your eyelashes and winks
Fooling around your beauty

History often unfolds
The secret truths
But always with a price

All the forgotten inks
All the scattered bloods
Bring us face to face

With those secret truths

Yet the closed-door meetings
Continue in security councils

And here I'm figuring out
Your smell, you doing the same
When blood overflows the ink

3rd December' 2019
Nilavronill Shoovro

Striving for Survival

Shadows of forgotten tears
Silent, remain mute spectators

Cleavages of upturned hopes
Agitating around age old debates

Rheumatic skeletons of dead warriors
With punctured memories and beliefs

Still hovering around the lost battles
Baffled, trying to resolve the conflicts

Yet the paratroopers of secret missions
Continue with their alluring dreams to sell

And here I am not to win your heart
Not to hurt it either, with betrayal

The roads ahead are yet to be paved
With the flame of Spring and human touch

The battlefields are yet to be maned with
The poets and painters of next millennium

With the new-borns and new faces
With new ideas new sketches

Fragrance of love fragrance of life
Resurrection of beliefs resurrection of hopes

16th January' 2020
NilavroNil Shoovro

The Unborn Civilians

Strange words are whispering though
With the gentle breeze, perhaps to
Disturb my patience, serenity

Sometimes even the dreams
Of the disturbed nights, blurred
Yet uncompromising keep on taunting

I can still see the faces around….
The unborn civilians laughing at me
Making me more uncomfortable

Alphabets are not enough to decode
The strange words, remain locked
In the unfinished signatures

Nights may sleep in compromise
Yet blurred dreams will dance
In amusement and in mayhem

But, the unborn civilians
Can you decode the words?
Can you tame the dreams, without laughing?

20th April' 2019
NilavroNill Shoovro

After The Last Battle

It was a day I can remember still
Not any lone figure to be seen around
No sound around the eternal silence
Of the dead body, I knew so long,
So well and vivid in every detail

Even the southern wind was too timid
To break the silent corridors of silence
Hanging between the sky and earth
Like the mute spectators of tragedies
Troubled, yet to find out any clue or hope

Nobody had scheduled any funeral
There was nobody left either
Only the speechless morning sun
Shining forth out of habit only
Perplexed, didn't know what to do

Those two eyes like the dead stones
Remained open like the empty deserts
Even without any questions like any-
Age old hypothesis of war and peace,
Remained clam like the crucified cross

It was only that dead body with the
Lost soul of mine, was lying there
All alone, in that lonely field of lost battle
Like the dead stars of the distant galaxies
Nowhere to reach or to retreat anywhere…

19th January' 2020
NilavroNill Shoovro

Alone In Lonely Battles

Naked bones of lost hopes
Buried under false words
Of fabricated histories;
Remain sleepless every night
Like the mute spectators

Even walking alongside
Of their lost dreams
And beaten souls;
I, unlike the others
Feel defeated every day

Rulers cover up every thing
With their sweet lies, false words
Empty promises and fake hopes;
But I, unlike their stooges
Still holding my own battles

Almost like the phoenix
Truths will emerge again
In fresh flesh and stubborn bones;
Even after my death, if they
Defeat me alone in my lonely battle

14th January' 2020
NilavroNill Shoovro

Landscapes Without A View

Gradually the moon was unfolding
It's secret, like the new bride
With gentle stride soft and light

I was there just in front of my script
Facing the distant memories, as if
Looking through the looking glass

All through the silent corridors
Of the unspoken words of love
Dreams remain alive like dead statues

Landscapes without any view
Just like the vision of fossils
Blind, nowhere to turn around

All the pages of autobiography
Circled around lies and deceit
Unlike the moon unfolding the secret

26th January' 2020
NilavroNill Shoovro

In My Lone Crusade…

The shadows of boring companions
Always chattering around human patience
Like the never-ending deserts without much hope…

I can see them anywhere around the clock
From down memory lanes to schedule times
Of war and peace, innovations and prejudice…

The much-awaited words and lines, rhymes
Silent monologues or speech of prophet
Would remain mute spectators, even again…

I have seen those shadows, marching ahead
Along their stupid dreams, desire and beliefs
Like the blindfolded clowns hovering around…

The thinning shades of reasons and truths
Feeling shy and keep quiet in solitude
Like the beaten warriors in lost battles…

But I, even with my words and lines
With eyes open and ears to the grounds
Waiting for you, in my lone crusade…

31st January' 2020
NilavroNill Shoovro

Waiting for The Last Ritual

The rain
With its cosmic eyes
Keeps knocking
At the windowpane
Trembling with each step
With all her secrets
In every drop, one by one.

The evening
Was waiting for the
Magical rituals....
Like secret manuscripts
For her readers.
It was dark like prison cells.
Waiting in a row for the final sentence.

The room
Was empty with the silence
Of the graveyard,
Except for the legacy
Of my ancestral breath.
Bit by bit. Again, and again.
Like the experienced leopards,

Before the final hunt. Our time,
Past present and the future aspirants,
Like the prodigal epics of beliefs
Is waiting for the last ritual.

17th August 2014
NilavroNill Shoovro

BOOK 2

A Single Dream

I just can say to you
All my silences
Are dancing through

This day and the days before
Till the last day ends
      I know it is you

This world with all its colours
Whispers around me
      Nothing but only one name

I just know how nice it is
To dream around one single dream
      For nothing but to feel alive

This day and the days before
Till the last day ends
      I know how much it is true

This world through all its epics
Has waited long enough
      To see you blush in my name…

31st October' 2019
NilavroNill Soovro

After The Fifteenth Step…

Watching the full moon
Coming out of the monsoon cloud
-In the middle of the lonely night

After the downpour
The sky seems to be smiling
Like her eyes

Shining bright and vivid
In our midnight paradise
Her eyes; brimming over in ecstasy

These sleepless nights
Bring her memories back
Not in pain nor in consolation

I can still count her steps
One, two…three… And the Fifteenth
Before she drove off

NilavroNill Shoovro

An Evening In Paris

Clouds were sailing through
With scattered rains now and then
Her eyes were full in tears
Like the faint moon beyond heaven

Traffic was heavy down the roads
With busy signals here and there
She had unbuttoned her silence
With her secret tales of affairs

The city was busy with the crowd
Mesmerized with the moments, ever
Her stories were unfolding like epics
With the pain of the sufferings forever

The city was bathed in rainbow
The evening was alive in joy
I was listening to her heartfelt
Not just like the heavenly envoy

With the dusk settling in time
Around the city everywhere
I found the syllables of love
Like the moon over the midnight…

14th May '2019
NilavroNill Shoovro

Almost Like The Fairy-tales …..

Beyond the stellar rays of mutual hopes
We knew each other well just like
The monsoon clouds and the rain drops
Sailing over the sky during heavy downpours

Days were like the fulfilment of dreams
With our mutual touches beyond limbs
All our words were jubilant in listening
Each other's syllable sailing around

All our peaceful melodies lyrical passions
Like the moonlight over the oceans
Were rhythmic dancing ever in reflection
Space and reality became time and eternity in love………

23rd September' 2018
NilavroNill Shoovro

Anonymous Dreams

Whenever you come in the dreams
With silent steps or tuned in
With the absorbing summer music
I don't know why or how
I don't know for what or for whom
I feel pangs deep inside down the
Memory lane,

Memories can be like the faded pages
Of forgotten histories, the fallen leaves
On the grass up-turned mute in grief

The dead colors and the lost words
Torn in shreds with muted whispers
May suffer still with your footsteps

I don't know where to find solace
I don't know how to mute your steps
I don't know for whom you step in
To invade anonymous dreams
Like the tyrants to rule
Like the rulers to conquer
Like the conquerors to thrive…..

28th September' 2019
NilavroNill Shoovro

Between Insanity And Hope

Still I can smell her perfumes
Different with the changes of her moods
Like the changing shades of her looks
With different stories in between

Still I can see her dancing
With arms clinging around her lovers
Steps in and steps out in rhythm
With different scripts in between

Still I can hear her words
Decorated nicely like fairy tales
Driving the lovers crazy
With different tunes in between

Still I can feel her dilemma
Not sure of her choices
Swinging only like the pendulums
Between insanity and hope

11th November' 2018
NilavroNill Shoovro

Beyond All Beliefs And Oaths

In this strange evening, when
Memories of stone ages seem to
Dance through our veins
I think I believe in your beauty

Or else, our empty dreams
Would have remained silent
With frozen shadows, yes-
Like the lonely moon beyond

This deadly darkness around
And our engraved passions
Since time immemorial
Interlinked like the twins

Beyond the histories and
The prehistoric era, the same
Old stories with mirages
And dreams keep us beside

A woman and her man
Touching in between, bare foot
Beyond all beliefs and oaths
Mesmerized, imprisoned
        but alive still

16th May' 2019
NilavroNill Shoovro

Children of Paradise

This night with you and me
The pale moon
Besides the overtaking clouds
And the occasional drizzles
Here and there...

Our memories distant
And Closed
Even with the shadows of hope
And despair within our little fights
Like the children of Paradise

Time had played with us
Or we had spoiled it…
Yet tonight I can see you there
Alone with my memories
And here I'm with yours

The silent chords of sufferings
With all the strings of desires
Broken in shreds
With our names engraved on
The night is still unfolding dear…

August The 28th' 2018
NilavroNill Shoovro

Colours Of Love

For you for me the primordial atom
Has waited long, down memory lane

Evolving itself into the universe
Dancing around the galaxies and stars

Making the sun so warm in feelings
Shaping the earth round around love

Preparing all the flowers you like
Giving me chance to garland you with

For you for me the primordial atom
Has waited long, defying war and battles

Saving the earth after each catastrophe
With new hopes and seeds harbouring life

Encouraging the poets to write down the epics
In felicitation of love amidst human tragedies

Presenting us with this canvas of life
Dreaming, we would draw new colours of love

16th January' 2020
NilavroNill Shoovro

Forgetting...

Her moist lips with sensuous tenderness
Like the gentle breeze on the river bank
Welcomed my kiss

I had forgotten the dried memories
The deceptive smiles and the fugitive words
Like love and home

The shadows of the wounded souls
With the tales of ditched loves and, yes
Abandoned homes-

Were parachuting around us like the
Combat forces in the middle of
Our Rendezvous

Yet we came closer yet we embraced
Our needs and desires, the night was so deep
Sensational and inevitable

**13th October' 2019
NilavroNill Shoovro**

Forlorn Footprints

In between hope and despair
I have seen her eyes
Dancing through the lyrics…
Of her own schedules

And my fractured nights
With all the truths and memories
After so many years
Silently pray her name…

In between love and desire
I have dreamt her smile
Dancing through the lyrics…
Of her own schedules

And my blank verses
With those empty words
Voiceless cries and moans
Try to listen her footsteps…

In between life and death
I have read her lines
Dancing through the lyrics
Of her own schedules

And my lonely steps
With those long strides
Although nowhere to go
Count her forlorn footprints…

11th October' 2019
NilavroNill Shoovro

Frozen Distance

These moonless nights~
Stressed beyond lonely shores
With the lazy breeze
Neither happy nor complaining

Jealous conversations
Amidst hostile passions
Playing with futile memories
Often bring us closer…

Across everyday moments
Even beyond our time scales
Heart bleeds in melancholy
Drafting silence, drifting on

Behind the darkness no rainbows
To unveil her face or mine
Or the frozen distance in between
Dead Syllables of love continue…

18th November' 2019
Nilavronill Shoovro

In Absence of Her...

I remember
The frozen hopes
I remember
The lonely nights
I remember
The dark shadows
Of prolonged pains, painful;
Yet waiting for someone, like her

Birds are coming back
Dusk is settling down
Around their wings.
It's time to prepare
For the night and for love…

Days are numbered
And time puts limit.
Silence settles down
Around my words
In absence of her…

Endless passion
Dances through…
Fractured nights
Like voiceless mists
Circle around…

**13th November' 2019
NilavroNill Shoovro**

Last Drop of Your Tears

The room was empty till then
No more midnight dreams to be followed
All the secret touches have vanished
Only few forgotten pains remained

The wind was wailing around
Light was too dark
    …to shine around faith
Temperature was shivering

Around all the bitter truths
Even time was frozen down
    …standstill, when I entered
Only with our memories

The speechless moon was watching
My steps around the corner
Then I saw the last drop of your tears
Still then waiting for me alone

16th October' 2018
NilavroNill Shoovro

Living Within Dreams

Let's remain without words
Here in dreams
beyond the midnights
Facing each other calm and confident
With subtle smile in sparkling eyes
Like the fresh rays of dawn
Like the migrant birds
      into the unknown territories
Breathing like the hundred-meter runners
Before the take-off
Counting every second
Like the precious treasures
      tonight, facing each other

Let's remain silent
Brimming in confidence
      beyond the dreams
Touching each other warm and fresh
With flames in throbbing hearts
Like the summer winds
Like the rainbows
      covering the entire sky
Feeling like the painters on canvas
After the final touch
Something in common
A sense of relief with completeness
      tonight, touching each other

5th May 2019
NilavroNill Shoovro

Lovers Or Strangers

Beneath the midnight moon
Fervent touches of blind faith
Side by side of the
Mingling shadows of hope

Lovers or strangers
Imprisoned in flesh and blood
When history unfolds
It's palette of desire and design

Men and women
Lovers or strangers alike
Can only dance like puppets
Mesmerized by time immemorial

Echoes of love around your kiss
Or even my penetration deep inside
Like the decoding of the program
Designed not by us, lovers or strangers…

Beneath the midnight moon
Eternity revolves around
No matter how we define the words
Or even refine them……

1st April' 2019
NilavroNill Shoovro

Men In Love

I watched her swimming like a river
Between the banks of passion,
Rippling in joy and happiness

Perhaps dreaming for a boatman
Rowing along for thousand years
Floating on the course of oblivion

She was alone along her beauty and grace
Like the delicate sunrise dissolving the mist
All alone from time immemorial, everyday

I watched her every day, swimming around
With her words rhythmic and passionate
Throbbing like the lyrics of my poems

She was there with her heart pure and virgin
Along her fragrance of hope and beliefs
Like the fairy tales of paradise, eternal

And my nights with their watchful eyes
Sleepless, stubborn like the believers of god
Kept on praying, calling her in all probable names

3rd January' 2020
NilavroNill Shoovro

New Found Dawn

Let's put few words between you and me
Few important words of compassion
Of touching the novelty of each other

The songs of everyday schemes
With the usual notes of personal whims
May try to provoke us in between

Let's try to walk along the fallen leaves
With the murmuring whispers of their grief
Listening their own stories and experiences

I know, all the ongoing human dramas
With their scripted resolutions and humor
Will never accept anything beyond history

Let's plunge into the abyss of the silent wounds
With our lips alive and waltzing around
Like the universal dance of eternity

Even if our stubborn ego hovering upon
May counter with age old hypothesizes
Ruining the gentle breeze of our new found dawn…

12th September; 2019
NilavroNill Shoovro

Not So Melancholic

All your footprints
One two three…..and so,
Burned right into my memories

The arrogance of your kisses
During our night odysseys
Your lips and the lipsticks

The fragrance of your words
Uttered so fervently
Assuring my private dreams

Everything skilfully articulated
In between the rhythmic dances
Of those seven minutes

Endless passions with wild laughter
Everything was so subtle
So mesmerizing in belief

That, even your graveyard
Celebrates our memories
With me around still

19th September' 2018
Nilavronill Shoovro

Penultimate Moment

Unknown steps of midnight chorus
Under the pale moon over the hill
Let's play with our hidden alphabets
Like the drummers of peace treaties

Silent words with impatient ears
Cool eyes like the leopards' walk
And we two facing each other's
Moist lips under control in wait

All the shapeless thoughts naked
And ashamed to reveal itself
Yet all our dreams centre around
Frozen hopes to win over

Voiceless shadows of bygone days
Dancing in the middle around
Alphabets of love and desire
Like the blind wind, circle us…

9th July '2019
NilavroNill Shoovro

On The Wings of Love

Whenever I see her eyes
Glittering in joy
And her fervent smile
Blinking like heavenly stars
    I know I am in love
        Flowing like the river
        Under the midnight moon
        Hoping for an ocean to open up

All the alphabets of human epics
All the songs to remember
All the memories of forgotten loves
Sing aloud her name
    Echoing around the morning breeze
    Dancing upon the sea waves
    Breaking the barriers of time and space
    Making the moments, eternal

Whenever I read her lines
Romantic and beaming in love
And her ardent words
Nursing the pains like God's will
    I know I am in love
        Standing amidst hope and despair
        At the bend of the road
        Hoping for her hands to touch…

All the silent desires and dreams
All the desperate hopes and likes
All the forlorn shadows of past
Write down her name
    Through the whispers of broken leaves
    Over the crescendos of water falls

On the wings of midnight sonata
Keeping me standstill in her wait…

3rd November' 2019
NilavroNill Soovro

Silent Tears

Whenever I read your poem
You don't know, but I feel you within
Every word counts, your alphabets
March forward, you don't know
Yes, through my heart crying in love
I can see you transparent
Circling around your rhymes,
The silent tears in crystal pain
Waiting for someone

Whenever I read your poem
You don't know, but I feel you within
Your tender heart throbbing in love
Like the sunflower waiting all night
For the dawn, tempting touch
Warm caring and soothing
Like the earth lying in draught
Dreaming the monsoon rain, and you
Waiting for someone

Whenever I read your poem
You don't know, but I feel you within
Like the iron ore around magnets
Like the river roaring ahead
To dive deep into the ocean
Like the dead souls waiting
For resurrection once again
You don't know, still I am
Waiting for someone like you

Whenever I read your poem
You don't know, but I feel you within
In my rendezvous with my dreams

The stretched nights of loneliness
The single moon hovering around
Dreams die fast in lost sentences
Of unwritten love, of silent tears
Yet every moment counts
Waiting for someone like you

**28th April' 2019
NilavroNill Shoovro**

Since Eternity

He was dwelling in utopia
Yes, he was designing his destiny
And he was the curator of his dreams
Loving caring with full of new ideas

Then she came, not with ideas
Not with any dream or design
She came like the fresh air
Like the water splash, refreshing

She came with passion
Blue eyes full of affection
Warm and comforting
Blooming in joy like flowers

He was watching her closely
Trying to classify her movements
Evaluating his own theories
Examining like true scientists

She was truly amazed, wondering
Curiosity in her own eyes
Watching him with care
Perhaps like God watching us…

      Since eternity…

29th July' 2019
NilavroNill Shoovro

The Broken Strings

In between the frozen kisses
I try to remember
Few intimate words along with
Those unfinished sentences…..

Like the untamed moon
Looming large behind the landscape
After the fresh shower
I try to remember everything

Unknown chorus of dead lovers…
Alphabets of the bygone oaths...
Even the dark shadows of mating time…
Along with the time scale

The broken strings of blind faiths
Scattered beyond my reach
Yet I try to mend few intimate words
In between those unfinished sentences…

9th' September 2018
Nilavronill Shoovro

The Invitation

The rain-soaked night
Under the dead stars
Of prehistoric age
Drenched and quiet
Like the hermits of the
Monastery in meditation
Dark as the dead faces
Of the warriors
In the lost battlefields

I don't know how to
Invite you in a night
Like this, deep in seclusion
This silent sky above
Beyond the midnight
Without desire and passions
The cold breeze over
The river whispering
Like the dead souls

Wild clouds with the
Raindrops thundering
Down, gone over the hills
If the midnight sonata
Wish to reveal our story
Would you like to join?
Like the shadows of the past
With the fragrance of joy
Painting the canvas of love

25th May' 2019
NilavroNill Shoovro

The Lazy Nights

Outside our everyday kisses
There was an old story
Without any beginning

From the cosmic truth
Towards our mutual lies
Days ahead and days beyond

She was there like every night
Playing rituals with my penis
Before preparing herself for me

And I the eternal fucker
Working with my fingers
Along her finer lines

We stood naked side by side
Wrapped only with our lies, even
The night was too lazy to watch us…

**22nd October' 2018
NilavroNill Shoovro**

The Lost Words

Somehow somewhere
I have lost my words
Even the synonyms
Are gone with them
I wish to call you back
But syllables remain silent

It is almost like walking
Through the desert sands
Where words and sentences
Have no purpose at all
Only the sky will drop down
To touch the silent sand

How can I call you back?
Even if I feel you inside
Wish to see you looking
At me eagerly, smiling
To listen my heart
Defying everything else!

No words no sentence
To help me out
How can I reach you?
How can you listen
My heart counting
Your footsteps ever?

This night silent pains
Watching every moment
Searching for own words
Amidst the ruins of hope
At least for a single

Sentence, I love you, Yes

With the silence echoing
Over all directions
In your name, scything
The nights all around
Wouldn't you find my words?
Lost, but not dumb yet…...

6th May' 2019
NilavroNill Shoovro

The Podium of Reunion

Strange smile of silent words
Muted voice of stark memories
During rendezvous with someone
Of fractured fidelity speaks volume

Faithless touches of mutual kisses
Age old hypotheses of stolen love
Sometimes pave smooth passage
To step in to the podium of reunion

Sharing dreams on everyday canvas
With blank faces and secret whims
Needs magical coordinates to unfold
New histories with scripted chapters

All the broken pieces of beliefs
All the stolen moments of desires
All the silenced words of love
May watch the curtain to be raised…

6th October '2019
NilavroNill Shoovro

The Silent Oath

She remained silent
Just like mountain
Feels comfort in it's
Own seclusion…

With her closed eyes
Perhaps like the
Ancient hermits
She was in meditations

Still all my songs
With the music of love
Tainted with pain
Will follow her silence

I can now feel everything
Fallen leaves of the winter
Broken chords of music
Mosaic of death wishes…

26th November' 2019
NilavroNill Shoovro

The Unfinished Signatures

like the blinking eyes
of a soft heart,
the maiden stars
were preparing for the night
i was trying very hard
yes, in my desolate exile
to draw her sketch
with few words of
love and sympathy
passions and desperations

like the mystery
of the fairy tales
the night was unfolding
it's purpose
i was trying to figure out
her footsteps, silent calm
yet confident in giving me
a surprise, I would like

like the roaring waves
of the oceans dancing naked
to waltz around with the shore
i was in my dream
to uphold my song
of a forlorn soul
for an engaging night
of the stars blinking still
for an epic to stage
amidst the ruins of the hopes

like the unknown dewdrops
of the forgotten nights

my songs dissolved
in pains and grief
her sketch remained
hazy in doubts and disbeliefs
frozen kisses remained dumb
with the unfinished signatures …

20th April' 2019
NilavroNill Shoovro

The Silent Ringtone

Like the Mediterranean sky
Whenever she looks through
Roaring waves of Atlantic
Seems to vibrate through veins

Like the morning breeze
Fresh and inspiring
All her good morning wishes
Keep me alive still

Rhythm of my lonely nights
Dark as the forlorn graveyards
Wait for her call, the ringtone
Never buzz, yet vibrates though

Like the silent whispers
Of the dead souls calling the
Dear ones in the middle of the
Nightmares for a fresh dawn…

21st November' 2019
NilavronIll Shoovro

The Unspoken Love

sharing the dreams…
even the blank faces
feel the voiceless words
something worthwhile

escaping from the agonies
running towards the exit
even the hopeless moments
become nostalgic

scanning the false prejudices
even the angry textures
seem to be proud enough
for the bygone memories

i know, if we come across
even again even if like the strangers
all the unspoken words
would merge into eternity…

7th November' 2018
NilavroNill Shoovro

Under The Forgotten Bridge

Under the forgotten bridge
The dusk is falling fast
Like the music of dew drops
In between our mutual hopes

Measuring each and every word
Emphatically in our solitude
Before forming any promise
Before taking any oath

Mirages are hypnotic we know
Like the utterance of love
Nothingness is even far better
Not the broken wings of dove

The dusk is falling now faster
Under the forgotten bridge
Eyes are patient like vultures
Here we are waiting still….

8th'September 2018
Nilavronill Shoovro

Unsigned Epitaph

Colour of footprints in between
Insanity and memories
With frozen desires
Like the music
Of the broken chords

Beyond the passions or pain
Over the rivulets of desperations
Still love sustains like the dead souls
Hovering around the burial
Waiting for someone

Countless moments in ashtrays
Even without any hope
Even without any scope
Like the burning charcoal
Feel you still, expecting nothing

All the dead nights, black and white
All the scattered words empty and void
All the torn sketches faded out
Replicate epics, over the pain
Over the unsigned epitaph

27th April' 2019
NilavroNill Shoovro

Waiting for Someone

Whenever I read your poem
You don't know, but I feel you within
Every word count, your alphabets
March forward, you don't know
Yes, through my heart crying in love
I can see you transparent
Circling around your rhymes,
The rhythmic tears in crystal pain
Waiting for someone

Whenever I read your poem
You don't know, but I feel you within
Your tender heart throbbing in love
Like the sunflower waiting all night
For the dawn, tempting touch
Warm caring and soothing
Like the earth lying in draught
Dreaming the monsoon rain, and you
Waiting for someone

Whenever I read your poem
You don't know, but I feel you within
Like the iron ore around magnets
Like the river roaring ahead
To dive deep into the ocean
Like the dead souls waiting
For resurrection once again
You don't know, still I am
Waiting for someone like you

Whenever I read your poem
You don't know, but I feel you within
In my rendezvous with my dreams

The stretched nights of loneliness
The single moon hovering around
Dreams die fast in lost sentences
Of unwritten love, of silent tears
Yet every moment counts
Waiting for someone like you

28th April' 2019
NilavroNill Shoovro

Waiting In The Dusk

With the rose in the right hand
She was waiting
At the door
Everything was arranged

As she knew his tastes
Likes and the prejudices
Like the descending dusk
After a busy schedule

Meeting with her smiling
All around brimming in ecstasy
Touching and hugging
Comforting each other

So it had to be dusk
With the return journey of the birds
After a hectic schedule
With her waiting at the door for him

The single flower in her hand
Was counting the time also
Keeping itself fresh in fragrance
To overwhelm the lovers in time

The clock on the side wall
Was blinking also now and then
For him to arrive soon
Keeping pace with her heartbeats

The table was laid down in advance
For an early dinner
With the decorations all around

To extend the comfort zone

And still then she was waiting
For him in love
Like the fragrance of roses
In the descending dusk

22^{nd'} August 2018
NilavroNill Shoovro

Yet The Debate Continues

It is dusk
Not yet dark
Like the north sky
Stars are preparing
For the evening conference

She will walk along with her love
At anytime for their rendezvous
With a red rose in one hand
The other hand will remain free

Although the evening is special
Also for the stars
As they are gearing up
For the heated debate

The lovers have no idea
About these developments
They are so composed
In their secrecy

Eyes remain locked
Desires are dancing
With mutual understanding
They are so familiar with

Yet the debate
Continues without
Any conclusion
About love and desire

She is now glowing hot
The vowels start humming

Pages of histories-
Unfolding secret stories

It grows darker
Stars are now very agitated
She starts to unfold her alphabets
The primordial Womb
Will take over soon

30th' July 2018
NilavroNill Shoovro

You Don't know

With those two eyes
Breathing new horizons
You don't know
Need not have to know
As if just like the wings
Of the seagulls
Hovering on and on
From time immemorial;
You keep me engaged
Days and nights in love

With your little steps
Paving new hopes
You don't know
Need not have to know
As if just like the dreams
Of the sailors
Rowing on and on
Discovering new found lands;
You keep me engaged
Days and nights in love

With your fervent smiles
Whenever you flash selfies
You don't know
Need not have to know
As if just like the sunrise
Of new dawns
Dissolving all around
The nights and darkness;
You keep me engaged
Days and nights in love

With my lines and curves
Working on my canvas
You don't know
Need not have to know
As if just like the pangs of
The forlorn rivers
Circling on and on
Waiting for weary Travellers;
My lines and curves dissolve
In voids days and nights

With my long strides
Covering time and space
You don't know
Need not have to know
As if just like the histories' of
Age old human tragedies
Playing on and on
Around beliefs and betrayals;
Long and weary strides crumble
In fatigues days and nights

With my solitary times
Listening only to silent heartbeats
You don't know
Need not have to know
As if just like the eternity
Of the outer space
Lamenting on and on
Around own loneliness;
My heart beats around
Your silence days and nights

29th November' 2019
NilavroNill Shoovro

CONTENTS

BOOK 1

Dreams Die Fast / 9
The Birth / 11
The Deep Secret / 13
Fragments of Revolutions / 15
Down Memory Lane / 16
When We Dance Together / 17
The Dark Passages / 18
After The Holocaust / 19
Back To Square One / 20
Before The Revolution / 21
End of The Civilization / 22
For The Next Millennium / 24
Denying The Graveyard / 26
None To Face The Trial / 27
Opera of The Gods / 28
Song of The Palestine / 29
The 21st Century Syndrome / 30
The Fight / 31
The Promised Land / 32
The Proposal / 33
Waiting For A Miracle / 34
With The Soul Face To Face / 35
A Woman Or A Poetry Line / 36
Around The Corner of Eternity / 37
Footprints of The Revolution / 38
Beneath The Treasure Mountains / 39
Dialects of Evolution / 41
Inside The Borders / 43
Last Words / 44
Lying Dead As Usual / 45
Not To Wake Up Anymore / 47
Preparing for A Duet Concert / 49

Of Human History / 50
Soldiers' Paradise / 51
The Rebellion / 52
The Price / 53
Striving for Survival / 55
The Unborn Civilians / 56
After The Last Battles / 57
Alone In Lonely Battles / 58
Landscape Without A View / 59
In My Lone Crusade / 60
Wating for The Last Ritual / 61

BOOK 2

A Single Dream / 65
After The Fifteen Steps / 66
An Evening In Paris / 67
Almost Like The Fairy-tales / 68
Anonymous Dreams / 69
Between Insanity And Hope / 70
Beyond All Beliefs And Oaths / 71
Children of Paradise / 72
Colours of Love / 73
Forgetting / 74
Forlorn Footprints / 75
Frozen Distance / 76
In Absence of Her / 77
The Last Drop of Your Tears / 78
Living Within Dreams / 79
Lovers Or Strangers / 80
Men In Love / 81
New Found Dawn / 82
Not So Melancholic / 83
Penultimate Moment / 84
On The Wings of Love / 85

Silent Tears / 87
Since Eternity / 89
The Broken Strings / 90
The Invitation / 91
The Lazy Nights / 92
The Lost Words / 93
The Podium of Reunion / 95
The Silent Oath / 96
The Unfinished Signatures / 97
The Silent Ringtone / 99
The Unspoken Love / 100
Under The Forgotten Bridge / 101
Unsigned Epitaph / 102
Waiting For Someone / 103
Waiting In The Dusk / 105
Yet The Debate Continues / 107
You Don't know / 109

EDITED BY ALICJA MARIA KUBERSKA

Awarded Polish poetess, novelist, journalist, editor. She writes both Polish and English. She is an author of many volumes. Her poems have been published in numerous anthologies and magazines in Poland, Czech Republic, the USA, the UK, Belgium, Bulgaria, Hungary, Albania, Spain, Argentina, Chile, Israel, Canada, India, Italy, Uzbekistan, South Korea, Taiwan and Australia. She won: medal on Nosside poetry competition in Italy, medal of European Academy Science, Arts and Letters in France, statuette in Lithuania. She was also twice nominated to the Pushcart Prize in the USA. Alicja Kuberska is a member of the Polish Writers Associations in Warsaw, Poland and IWA Bogdani, Albania. She is also a member of directors' board of Soflay Literature Foundation.

www.ingramcontent.com/pod-product-compliance
Lightning Source LLC
Chambersburg PA
CBHW031942070426
42450CB00005BA/437